CODING WIZARDS: A STEP-BY-STEP KIDS' GAME DESIGN GUIDE

Contents

3

4

Introduction:

Welcoming you to the exciting world of kid-friendly coding games! We will walk you through the steps necessary to create engaging and educational games that introduce children to the wonders of programming in this comprehensive guide. Coding isn't only for grown-ups — children can have a great time while creating significant abilities, for example, sensible reasoning, critical thinking, and imagination.

Whether you're an educator, a parent, or somebody energetic about motivating youthful personalities, this bit by bit guide will walk you through the method involved with creating intelligent and engaging games. We'll cover all that from characterizing learning objectives to choosing the right programming language and planning spellbinding game ideas.

As we leave on this experience, recall that the objective is to make learning fun. Toward the finish of this aide, you'll not just have a strong comprehension of how to make coding games customized for youngsters yet additionally the fulfillment of seeing youthful students investigate the wizardry of coding in a perky and creative manner.

In this way, we should make a plunge and open the capability of coding games as a passage to a reality where imagination meets innovation, and learning is a completely exhilarating experience!

Step 1: Define the Learning Objectives

Before beginning the process of developing coding games for children, it is essential to clearly define the learning objectives. The targets you set will shape the instructive experience and guarantee that the game gives important bits of knowledge into the universe of coding. This is the way to move toward this significant starting step:

1.1 Distinguish Target Age Gathering:

Decide the age bunch for which the game is planned. The children's interests and cognitive abilities will determine the learning objectives. Fitting your way to deal with a particular age range guarantees the substance is both open and testing.

1.2 Select Educational Goals:

Determine the key ideas or abilities you want your children to have. Whether it's comprehension fundamental programming builds, upgrading critical abilities to think, or encouraging innovativeness, obviously frame the instructive goals your game plans to accomplish.

1.3 Line up with Educational program (Discretionary):

Assuming the coding game is intended for instructive organizations, check in the event that there are explicit educational plan norms you can line up with. This guarantees that the game supplements homeroom learning and gives a consistent mix of coding abilities.

1.4 Encourage 21st Century Abilities:

Think about more extensive abilities fundamental in the computerized age, like decisive reasoning, coordinated effort, and correspondence. Your game can act as a stage to support these 21st-century abilities, getting ready children for an innovation driven future.

1.5 Equilibrium Challenge and Tomfoolery:

Make progress toward a harmony between instructive difficulties and diversion. The growth opportunity ought to be connecting with, inspiring children to investigate coding ideas while having some good times. The learning journey can be made more exciting by including a storyline or game narrative.

1.6 Measure Progress:

Characterize how you will evaluate and quantify the advancement of the students. This could incorporate following finished levels, effective critical thinking, or the dominance of explicit coding abilities. Obvious signs of progress support proceeded with commitment.

1.7 Think about inclusion:

Guarantee that the learning objectives are comprehensive and take care of different learning styles. Consider integrating components that enticement for visual, hear-able, and sensation students, making the coding experience open to a different gathering of children.

By carefully characterizing your learning objectives, you establish the groundwork for a coding game that charms youthful personalities as well as gives an organized and successful opportunity for growth. How about we continue on toward the following stage and pick the right programming language to rejuvenate your instructive game.

Step 2: Pick a Programming Language

Choosing a suitable programming language is a vital stage in making coding games for youngsters. The decision of language ought to line up with the age bunch, learning objectives, and in general instructive methodology. A guide to selecting the appropriate programming language is provided below:

2.1 Evaluate Target Age and Ability Level:

Consider the age and expertise level of your interest group. For more youthful youngsters, visual and block-based programming dialects like Scratch may be more reasonable, giving a fun loving and instinctive prologue to coding ideas.

Text-based programming languages like Python and JavaScript may be beneficial for older children with more advanced cognitive abilities.

2.2 Visual versus Text-Based Dialects:

Choose whether a visual or text-based language is more fitting. Visual dialects are in many cases more captivating for fledglings, permitting them to move code blocks. Text-based dialects give a more customary coding experience and might be reasonable for more established children or those with some coding experience.

2.3 Openness and Assets:

Assess the accessibility of learning assets and backing for the picked language. The process of learning can be greatly facilitated by robust online communities, tutorials, and educational platforms. Consider dialects with an abundance of assets explicitly intended for showing kids how to code.

2.4 Instructive Stages:

Investigate programming languages supported by educational platforms. A structured approach to coding education is provided by platforms like Scratch, Code.org, and Tynker, which are designed specifically for young learners.

2.5 Game Improvement Libraries:

On the off chance that the objective is to present game improvement ideas, pick a language that has reasonable game advancement libraries. For instance, Pygame for Python or p5.js for JavaScript are incredible decisions for making intuitive games.

2.6 Long haul Appropriateness:

Think about the drawn out appropriateness of the picked language. While early on dialects like Scratch are fantastic for novices, changing to an all the more generally utilized language like Python or JavaScript can give a smoother way to future learning and certifiable applications.

2.7 Connecting with and Fun Components:

Prioritize languages that enable you to incorporate fun and engaging gameplay elements. Special visualizations, livelinesss, and intuitive elements can upgrade the general opportunity for growth and keep kids spurred.

2.8 Think about Instructor/Parent Commonality:

Assuming that the game is planned for instructive settings, think about the commonality of educators or guardians with the picked language. Picking a language that instructors are OK with can work with better help for students.

Via cautiously considering these elements, you can pick a programming language that lines up with the instructive objectives of your game and gives a charming and successful growth opportunity for youngsters. You will be prepared to begin the exciting process of designing the game concept once the language has been chosen. Move on to Step 3 now!

Step 3: A crucial step in developing

A children's coding game is developing the game concept. This stage includes forming the story, characters, and difficulties to make the growth opportunity both pleasant and instructive. This is an aide en route to plan a convincing game idea:

3.1 Define the Goal of the Game:

Clearly state your game's educational objective. Whether it's presenting fundamental programming ideas, upgrading critical thinking abilities, or cultivating inventiveness, having an obvious reason will direct the general plan.

3.2 Lay out a Storyline:

Create a compelling narrative that seamlessly incorporates coding challenges. The story can give setting to the coding assignments, making the growth opportunity more vivid. Consider utilizing interesting characters and a plot that resounds with the objective age bunch.

3.3 Characters and Setting:

Foster characters that are both interesting and drawing in for youngsters. Think about the game's setting — whether it's a fantastical world, space, or a verifiable time. The characters and laying out ought to supplement the instructive objectives and improve the general allure of the game.

3.4 Identify Obstacles in Coding:

Coordinate coding difficulties into the storyline. These difficulties ought to line up with the learning objectives characterized in Sync 1. Create a storyline in which characters must use loop structures to navigate a maze, for instance, if the objective is to teach loops.

3.5 Progressive Intricacy:

Configuration levels with a progressive expansion in intricacy. Begin with straightforward coding undertakings and logically present further developed ideas. This guarantees that the game is available for novices while giving open doors to authority and development.

3.6 Integrate Intuitiveness:

Make the game fun and interactive. Coding allows players to interact with the characters and the environment. Integrate components like movements, audio effects, and criticism to establish a dynamic and vivid learning climate.

3.7 Incorporate Critical thinking Situations:

Present critical thinking situations inside the game. Urge children to utilize coding abilities to conquer difficulties and riddles. This supports coding ideas as well as advances decisive reasoning.

3.8 Equilibrium Schooling and Amusement:

Work out some kind of harmony between instructive substance and diversion. The game ought to be agreeable for youngsters while conveying important opportunities for growth. Think about including things that make learning seem like a fun and exciting adventure.

3.9 Iterative Plan:

Be available to iterative plan. Test the game idea with a little gathering of children and assemble criticism. Utilize this input to refine and work on the game idea, guaranteeing that it resounds with the main interest group.

3.10 Openness and Inclusivity:

Make sure that the game's concept is understandable to a wide range of people. To make the game appealing to a wide range of kids, take language, cultural sensitivity, and inclusivity into consideration.

You set the stage for an educational and entertaining coding experience by carefully designing the game's concept. When your idea is hardened, now is the right time to set up the advancement climate and begin rejuvenating your game in Sync 4.

Step 4: Set Up the Advancement Climate

Setting up the improvement climate is a critical step that guarantees you have the fundamental devices and programming to begin coding your game. Contingent upon the programming language picked in Sync 2, the arrangement cycle might differ. Here is a general manual for assist you with setting up the improvement climate for coding games for youngsters:

4.1 Pick an Incorporated Advancement Climate (IDE) or Stage:

Select an IDE or stage that upholds the picked programming language. Here are a few models:

Scratch Online Manager: Assuming you're utilizing Scratch, basically visit the Scratch online manager (scratch.mit.edu) to begin making your game. No extra arrangement is required.

Thonny for Python: Thonny is a fledgling accommodating Python IDE. Download and introduce Thonny from thonny.org. It accompanies an underlying Python mediator and improves on the coding system.

Code.org or Tynker: Children can learn to code on these online platforms. Explore the coding environments at code.org and tynker.com with an account.

Word processors and Programs for JavaScript: On the off chance that you're utilizing JavaScript, you can utilize a word processor like Visual Studio Code or even the implicit code proofreader in internet browsers. Basically make a HTML record and begin coding.

4.2 Introduce Vital Libraries or Expansions:

Assuming that you're utilizing a programming language that requires extra libraries or expansions for game turn of events, try to introduce them. For instance:

Pygame for Python: On the off chance that you're making games in Python utilizing Pygame, introduce Pygame by running pip introduce pygame in the terminal or order brief.

p5.js for JavaScript: For JavaScript game turn of events, incorporate the p5.js library in your HTML record. You can get it from p5js.org or use a content distribution network (CDN).

4.3 Look into the Climate:

Find opportunity to investigate the highlights of the picked improvement climate. Comprehend how to make new activities, open existing ones, and explore the point of interaction. Experience with the climate will make the coding system smoother.

4.4 Set Up Client Records (if relevant):

Create user accounts for both you and the children who will be using online platforms like Scratch, Code.org, or Tynker. This permits you to handily save and offer tasks.

4.5 Access Documentation and Assets:

Investigate the available documentation and resources for the selected environment. This could include forums, tutorials, and guides where you can get advice and ideas as you make your game.

4.6 Actually take a look at Similarity:

Guarantee that the advancement climate is viable with the gadgets the children will utilize. Whether it's work areas, PCs, or tablets, confirm that the coding climate works consistently on the expected stages.

4.7 Set Up Form Control (Discretionary):

Consider utilizing adaptation control devices like Git to follow changes in your code. This is particularly valuable in the event that different individuals are teaming up on the undertaking or on the other hand to track your advancement.

By setting up the improvement climate, you lay the foundation for a smooth coding experience. With everything set up, you're prepared to plunge into the thrilling system of learning and executing essential programming ideas in your game.

Continue to Stage 5 to begin coding
and rejuvenate your game!

Step 5: Get familiar with the Fundamentals of Programming

Prior to jumping into coding your game, having a strong comprehension of the fundamentals of programming is fundamental. Whether you're utilizing a visual language like Scratch or a text-based language like Python, it is critical to embrace central ideas. Here is an aide on learning the rudiments:

5.1 Grasp Factors:

Definition: Factors are holders for putting away information values.

Example: In Scratch, make a variable to store the score in a game. In Python, use factors to store values like player names or scores.

5.2 Investigate Information Types:

Definition: Information types characterize the sort of information a variable can hold.

Example: In Python, there are information types like int (whole number), str (string), and float (drifting point number). Comprehend how to utilize these information types in your code.

5.3 Handle Control Designs:

Definition: Control structures, similar to circles and conditionals, deal with the progression of a program.

Example: Utilize a circle to rehash a bunch of activities in Scratch or Python. Carry out conditionals to settle on choices in light of game occasions.

5.4 Learn Capabilities and Techniques:

Definition: Reusable code is made up of blocks like procedures and functions.

Example: In Scratch, make custom blocks to typify code that performs explicit assignments. In Python, characterize capabilities to coordinate and reuse code.

5.5 Take Event-Driven Programming into Account:

Definition: In occasion driven programming, code answers explicit occasions or client activities.

Example: In Scratch, you can use events to set off actions when a sprite is clicked or a certain condition is met. In Python, comprehend how to deal with occasions utilizing libraries like Pygame.

5.6 Work on Troubleshooting:

Definition: Troubleshooting includes distinguishing and fixing blunders in your code.

Example: Purposefully bring mistakes into your code and work on troubleshooting. Comprehend normal blunder messages and how to investigate issues.

5.7 Investigate Information and Result:

Definition: Input alludes to client connections, and result is the consequence of a program's execution.

Example: Utilize mouse or keyboard events for input in Scratch. In Python, investigate input capabilities to get client info and print explanations for yield.

5.8 Adhere to Best Coding Practices:

Definition: Coding best practices further develop code coherence and practicality.

Example: Make use of meaningful variable names, include comments to explain intricate sections, and adhere to standard indentation. Build up the significance of clearness in coding.

5.9 Use Online Assets:

Definition: Influence online instructional exercises, documentation, and intuitive coding works out.

Example: Investigate coding stages like Code.org, Khan Foundation, or intelligent coding sites to build up how you might interpret programming ideas.

5.10 Work together and Look for Help:

Definition: Joint effort and looking for help are fundamental parts of the growing experience.

Example: Join internet coding networks, gatherings, or nearby coding clubs. Share your difficulties and gain from others.

By dominating these central programming ideas, you'll be better prepared to handle the coding difficulties in your game. Presently, we should continue on toward Stage 6 and begin carrying out these ideas to make the groundwork of your coding game for youngsters.

Step 6: Begin with Basic Models

Since you have a strong comprehension of the rudiments of writing computer programs, now is the ideal time to try that information by making straightforward models. Beginning with direct coding activities will assist you with building the establishment for the more complicated parts of your game. This is an aide en route to start:

6.1 Pick Fundamental Coding Activities:

Select straightforward coding practices that line up with the learning objectives of your game. For instance, make a program that moves a person on the screen, changes tones, or answers client input.

6.2 Execute Factors and Information Types:

Data can be stored and manipulated with variables. Practice working with integers, strings, and floats, among other data types. Create a program, for instance, that tracks a player's score.

6.3 Analysis with Control Designs:

Carry out control structures like circles and conditionals. Make a program that rehashes an activity utilizing a circle or settles on choices in view of specific circumstances.

6.4 Investigate Capabilities and Methods:

Work on characterizing and utilizing capabilities or techniques. Divide your code into blocks that can be used again and again. Create a function, for instance, that controls player movement or animates a character.

6.5 Incorporate Occasion Driven Programming:

Explore different avenues regarding occasion driven programming. Foster a basic program where activities are set off by unambiguous occasions, for example, a vital press or mouse click.

6.6 Troubleshoot and debug:

Demonstrate your ability to debug when you encounter intentional code errors. Figure out how to recognize normal issues and use troubleshooting apparatuses accessible in your picked programming climate.

6.7 Add Essential Info and Result:

Remember fundamental info and result highlights for your models. This could include getting client input or showing data on the screen. For example, make a program that asks the player for their name.

6.8 Test and Emphasize:

Test your straightforward models completely. Distinguish any issues or enhancements required and emphasize on your code. This iterative interaction refines your programming abilities.

6.9 Utilize Online Stages and Instructional exercises:

Investigate internet coding stages and instructional exercises to track down directed works out. Sites like Code.org, Scratch, or intelligent coding stages offer an assortment of novice well disposed works out.

6.10 Offer and Look for Input:

Share your basic models with others, particularly your interest group. Gather input to comprehend how connecting with and justifiable your code is for youngsters.

Beginning with straightforward models supports your programming abilities as well as fabricates the foundation for the more complicated parts of your game. When you're OK with these fundamental ideas, you're prepared to continue on toward the subsequent stage: incorporating game elements into your project to code. The seventh step is just around the corner!

Step 7: Integrate Game Elements

Now that you have practiced coding by using straightforward examples, it is time to move on to incorporating game elements into your project. This includes rejuvenating your game idea by consolidating characters, difficulties, and associations. This is an aide en route to coordinate these game components:

7.1 Execute Characters:

Bring characters into your game. Characterize their attributes, appearances, and jobs. In Scratch, make sprites for your characters, and in Python or JavaScript, use pictures or shapes to address them.

7.2 Plan the Game Climate:

Set up the game climate, including foundations and settings. Think about the visual elements that go well with your story. In Pygame or p5.js, make a material or screen to act as the game climate.

7.3 Characterize Collaborations:

Indicate how characters associate with one another and the climate. Determine the game's actions that set off events. For instance, make characters move, hop, or answer explicit orders.

7.4 Create Obstacles:

Include obstacles and challenges that are compatible with your learning objectives. Make coding tasks that require you to be able to solve problems. Difficulties can go from exploring a labyrinth to tackling puzzles utilizing coding ideas.

7.5 Use Activitys and Impacts:

Add livelinesss and special visualizations to make the game more unique. Make sprite activitys or use advances to improve the general insight. Visual criticism makes the coding system really captivating.

7.6 Incorporate Sound:

Improve the game with audio effects and ambient sound. In Scratch, add sound blocks to set off sound occasions. Incorporate sound libraries into Pygame or p5.js to bring your game to life acoustically.

7.7 Execute Scorekeeping:

Acquaint scorekeeping components with track player progress. Use factors to store and refresh scores in view of in-game accomplishments. This builds up the idea of factors and information the executives.

7.8 Test and Investigate Constantly:

As you incorporate new components, test your game

frequently. Distinguish and troubleshoot any issues that emerge during testing. Guaranteeing the smooth usefulness of your game components is essential for a positive client experience.

7.9 Equilibrium Trouble Levels:

Try to achieve a difficulty curve that is even. Steadily increment the intricacy of difficulties to give a pride as players progress. An even game keeps students inspired.

7.10 Request Client Criticism:

Share your game with the interest group and accumulate criticism. Comprehend how children collaborate with the game, what they view as trying or pleasant, and utilize this data to refine and work on your plan.

Incorporating game components into your coding project is an intriguing stage where your underlying ideas begin coming to fruition. As you refine and clean these components, you draw nearer to making an instructive and engaging coding game for youngsters. Stage 8 will direct you in upgrading the visual and hearable allure of your game by adding illustrations and sound.

Step 8: Add Illustrations and Sound

Adding illustrations and sound to your coding game is a critical step that upgrades the visual and hearable allure of the general insight. Kids can have a more enjoyable and immersive learning experience when engaging visuals and sound effects are used. This is an aide en route to add designs and sound to your game:

8.1 Make or Pick Visual Resources:

Plan or select visual resources like characters, foundations, and items. In Scratch, utilize the underlying sprite library or make custom sprites. For Python (Pygame) or JavaScript (p5.js), you can utilize visual computerization programming or find free resources on the web.

8.2 Coordinate Visual Components:

Carry out visual components into your game. Put characters on the screen, set foundations, and add other graphical components. Think about utilizing livelinesss to make characters and items more powerful.

8.3 Carry out Visual Criticism:

Utilize visual feedback to symbolize interactions or events. For instance, change the shade of a person when it finishes a job or add enhanced visualizations when a level is finished. Visual criticism supports the circumstances and logical results relationship in coding.

8.4 Integrate Audio cues:

Coordinate audio effects to go with in-game occasions. Appoint explicit sounds to activities like person developments, collaborations, or level fruitions. This adds a hearable aspect to the growth opportunity.

8.5 Present Ambient sound:

Add some background music to your game to change the mood. Pick music that supplements the subject and temperament of your game. Guarantee that the volume levels are fitting and not diverting.

8.6 Use Text and Marks:

Incorporate text and names to give guidelines, data, or criticism inside the game. In Scratch, utilize the "say" block, and in Python or JavaScript, consolidate text delivering to show data on the screen.

8.7 Test Illustrations and Sound:

Test the illustrations and sound parts of your game completely.

Guarantee that visual components are shown accurately, liveliness run as expected, and audio effects play at the perfect opportunities. Address any issues that emerge during testing.

8.8 Improve for Execution:

Make sure your game runs smoothly by optimizing the graphics and sound files, especially if it will be played on multiple devices with different capabilities. Pack pictures and sound records without compromising quality.

8.9 Energize Customization (Discretionary):

If relevant, permit clients to tweak visual and hear-able components. For example, let players pick their personality's appearance or select their number one ambient sound. Customization adds an individual touch to the gaming experience.

8.10 Stick to the Same Theme:

Guarantee that illustrations, sound, and generally speaking plan keep a reliable topic all through the game. Consistency improves the general client experience and adds to a cleaned and proficient look.

Adding illustrations and sound isn't just about making the game outwardly engaging yet additionally about establishing a vivid and connecting with climate for learning. With these components set up, your coding game for youngsters is turning into a more intelligent and pleasant experience. Continue on toward Stage 9 to test and troubleshoot your game, guaranteeing that it capabilities true to form and gives a positive growth opportunity.

Step 9: Test and Investigate

Testing and troubleshooting are basic strides in the improvement cycle, guaranteeing that your coding game capabilities as expected and gives a positive growth opportunity. Exhaustive testing distinguishes and fix any issues, making the game seriously captivating and pleasant for youngsters. How to test and debug your coding game is as follows:

9.1 Test Every Part of the Game:

Direct thorough testing of every game component. Guarantee that characters move accurately, challenges are introduced as expected, and visual and hear-able components work consistently. Test each component to get likely issues.

9.2 Playtest with the Interest group:

Assemble a gathering of children from your interest group to playtest the game. See how they associate with the game, note any disarray or difficulties they face, and gather criticism on their general insight.

9.3 Identify issues and set priorities:

Report any bugs, errors, or issues experienced during testing. Focus on these issues in light of their effect on interactivity and the general client experience.

9.4 Investigating Instruments:

Use investigating instruments given by your programming climate. To find and fix errors, set breakpoints, examine variables, and walk through your code one line at a time. Influence print explanations for extra perceivability.

9.5 Blunder Dealing with:

Carry out mistake dealing with components to deal with startling circumstances effortlessly. Show educational messages or prompts to direct the player when mistakes happen. This upgrades the client experience and diminishes disappointment.

9.6 Test on Various Gadgets:

Assuming that your game is planned for different gadgets, test it on various stages and screen sizes. Guarantee that the game design, illustrations, and collaborations are advanced for every gadget.

9.7 Really take a look at Program Similarity:

Assuming that your game is electronic, check its similarity with various internet browsers. Test your game on famous programs like

Chrome, Firefox, Safari, and Edge to guarantee a steady encounter.

9.8 Screen Execution:

Watch out for the exhibition of your game. Check for any slack, stoppages, or memory issues, particularly as the game advances to additional intricate levels.

9.9 Location Client Input:

Include any user feedback as well as feedback from playtesting sessions. Address concerns, make enhancements, and emphasize on the game in light of the info you get.

9.10 Lead Iterative Testing:

Test iteratively as you fix problems and make changes. Test every cycle completely to guarantee that fixes or improvements don't present new issues.

9.11 Educational Effectiveness Test:

Assess the game's viability in gathering its instructive objectives. Survey whether the coding difficulties line up with the learning targets and assuming players are acquiring the expected information and abilities.

9.12 Beta Delivery (Discretionary):

Think about a beta delivery to a more extensive crowd. This can give important experiences from a bigger client base and assist with recognizing any unexpected issues before the authority discharge.

9.13 Record Changes:

Keep nitty gritty documentation of changes made during the testing and investigating process. This documentation is valuable for reference and can assist with following the development of your game.

By completely testing and investigating your coding game, you guarantee that it satisfies quality guidelines and gives an ideal growth opportunity to kids. You can proceed to Step 10 and finish your game before distributing it to the intended audience once you are satisfied with the testing phase.

Step 10: Archive and Offer

Archiving and sharing your coding game is fundamental for guaranteeing that others can figure out, use, and partake in the instructive experience you've made. Appropriate documentation helps instructors, guardians, and students explore the game and its instructive parts. This is an aide en route to record and share your coding game:

10.1 Produce User Manuals:

Foster client documentation that gives clear directions on the most proficient method to play the game. Include details about the game's objectives, controls, and any educational ideas that are covered. Use language appropriate for your ideal interest group.

10.2 Make sense of Learning Goals:

Obviously frame the learning targets and objectives of the game. Explain, if necessary, how the game complies with curriculum requirements or educational standards. Parents and educators need this information.

10.3 Give Investigating Tips:

Expect normal issues that players could experience and give investigating tips. Incorporate a FAQ segment or an investigating guide in your documentation to assist clients with beating difficulties.

10.4 Incorporate Game Screen captures:

Improve your documentation with screen captures that show key parts of the game. This visual portrayal helps with figuring out the connection point, interactivity, and coding difficulties.

10.5 Specify the requirements of the system:

Make it clear what your game's system requirements are. Incorporate data about the upheld gadgets, programs, or programming adaptations. This assists clients with guaranteeing their gadgets are viable.

10.6 Make a Game Instructional exercise (Discretionary):

Foster an intuitive instructional exercise inside the game or as a different asset. Users can learn about the game's basic features, controls, and educational aspects with the help of a tutorial.

10.7 Keep accessibility in mind:

Guarantee that your documentation is open to a different crowd. Utilize clear textual styles, decipherable text measures, and consider giving elective organizations to clients with explicit necessities.

10.8 Pick a Circulation Stage:

Choose a distribution channel for your game. This could be a site, an instructive stage, or a devoted space for coding projects. Stages like GitHub, Scratch, or committed instructive entrances are well known decisions.

10.9 Offer Instructive Assets:

Incorporate extra instructive assets that supplement the game. This could incorporate connections to coding instructional exercises, advantageous materials, or references that further build up the ideas presented in the game.

10.10 Support Input:

Urge clients to furnish criticism on their involvement in the game. Make an input structure or direct clients to a conversation gathering where they can share their contemplations, ideas, and experiences.

10.11 Influence Virtual Entertainment:

Make use of social media platforms to spread the word about your game to more people. Share updates, declarations, and examples of overcoming adversity to make a local area around your coding game.

10.12 Screen Utilization Examination:

On the off chance that conceivable, execute investigation instruments to screen how clients connect with your game. Investigating client conduct can give important bits of knowledge to future enhancements and updates.

10.13 Maintain Up-to-Date Documentation:

Consistently update your documentation to mirror any changes, increments, or upgrades to the game. This guarantees that clients approach the most recent data.

10.14 Observe Accomplishments:

Share stories of students' successes and celebrate their accomplishments. Feature outstanding undertakings or coding achievements to rouse others and grandstand the instructive effect of your game.

You contribute to the accessibility and success of your educational project by effectively documenting and sharing your coding game. This step makes way for proceeded with commitment and advancing inside the local area you've worked around your game. Congrats on arriving at this stage!

Step 11: Emphasize and Move along

Emphasizing and further developing your coding game is a urgent continuous interaction that permits you to upgrade the instructive experience, fix any issues, and adjust to client input. Your game will remain relevant, engaging, and in line with the requirements of your target audience if it goes through regular iterations. This is an aide while heading to repeat and further develop your coding game:

11.1 Gather Client Criticism:

Keep gathering client input from players, teachers, and guardians. The user experience, learning outcomes, and any areas that may require improvement are all revealed by this feedback.

11.2 Examine Analytics of Usage:

Assuming you've executed examination apparatuses, dissect use information to comprehend how clients cooperate with your game. Distinguish famous elements, client ways, and potential trouble spots to illuminate your iterative cycle.

11.3 Fix Problems and Bugs:

Check for and fix any bugs or problems that users report on a regular basis. Immediately delivering bug fixes adds to a positive client experience and keeps up with the honesty of the instructive substance.

11.4 Present New Difficulties:

Keep the substance new by presenting new coding difficulties or levels. Step by step increment the intricacy to take special care of the two novices and further developed students. Guarantee that the new difficulties line up with the general learning goals.

11.5 Upgrade Visuals and Sound:

Think about making the game's graphics and sound better or updating it. This can incorporate adding new designs, livelinesss, or audio cues to keep an outwardly engaging and vivid climate.

11.6 Extend Instructive Substance:

Investigate chances to extend the instructive substance of your game. Present new coding ideas, illustrations, or intelligent components that add to a more far reaching opportunity for growth.

11.7 Work with teachers to collaborate:

Team up with teachers to assemble experiences into the instructive viability of your game. Make adjustments in line with the game's alignment with classroom objectives and curriculum standards.

11.8 Advance for Availability:

Ceaselessly improve your game for openness. Guarantee that it stays usable by a different crowd, incorporating those with various capacities, foundations, and learning styles.

11.9 Screen Mechanical Updates:

Remain informed about updates and headways in the advances or stages you're utilizing. This incorporates updates to programming dialects, game advancement libraries, or online stages. Staying up with the latest guarantees similarity and security.

11.10 Draw in with the Local area:
Keep a functioning presence locally encompassing your game. Draw in with clients through gatherings, online entertainment, or different channels. Answer requests, recognize input, and celebrate client accomplishments.

11.11 Lead Occasional Assessments:
Lead occasional assessments of the game's instructive effect. Evaluate whether the learning objectives are being accomplished and on the off chance that clients are acquiring the expected information and abilities.

11.12 Arrangement Significant Updates:

Plan and execute significant updates to your game at normal stretches. These updates could incorporate huge substance extensions, new highlights, or upgrades to the general client experience.

11.13 Make Feature Requests Public:

Urge clients to submit highlight demands. Survey these solicitations in light of their arrangement with the instructive objectives and the practicality of execution. Client mentioned highlights can upgrade the game's significance.

11.14 Observe Achievements:

Commend achievements and accomplishments connected with your coding game. Recognize client achievements, feature examples of overcoming adversity, and utilize these achievements as any open doors to draw in with the local area. Your coding game's success depends on the continual iterative and improvement process. By constantly refining and growing your instructive undertaking, you add to a dynamic and powerful opportunity for growth for youngsters keen on coding. Congrats on your obligation to progressing improvement!

Step 12: Connect with the Local area

Connecting with the local area is a pivotal part of the achievement and manageability of your coding game. Building a local area around your instructive venture establishes a steady climate, encourages cooperation, and guarantees that your game remaining parts pertinent to the requirements of your crowd. This is an aide en route to connect with the local area really:

12.1 Lay out Internet based Presence:

Make and keep an internet based presence for your coding game. This could incorporate a committed site, online entertainment profiles, or a local area discussion where clients can interface and offer their encounters.

12.2 Web-based Entertainment Commitment:

Connect with your audience by using social media platforms. Share updates, declarations, and instructive substance connected with coding. Urge clients to impart their accomplishments and encounters to the game.

12.3 Local area Discussions or Gatherings:

Set up local area gatherings or gatherings where clients can examine the game, get clarification on pressing issues, and offer bits of knowledge. Stages like Conflict, Reddit, or devoted discussions on your site can work with local area collaboration.

12.4 Client Produced Content:

Urge clients to make and share their own coding ventures or adjustments of your game. Not only does user-generated content add value to the community, but it also demonstrates your audience's creativity.

12.5 Live Occasions and Online courses:

Arrange live occasions or online classes connected with coding, game turn of events, or instructive subjects. These occasions give a chance to coordinate collaboration with your local area and can include visitor speakers or coding difficulties.

12.6 Work with teachers to collaborate:

Team up with instructors to coordinate your game into instructive settings. Offer assets, example plans, or expert advancement potential open doors for educators. Drawing in with teachers reinforces the instructive effect of your game.

12.7 Feature Client Accomplishments:

Celebrate and feature client accomplishments inside the local area. Share examples of overcoming adversity, grandstand noteworthy coding projects, and recognize clients who have succeeded in learning through your game.

12.8 Back and forth Discussions:

Have normal round table discussions where clients can pose

inquiries about coding, game turn of events, or explicit difficulties inside your game. This makes an immediate line of correspondence and helps address client questions.

12.9 Criticism Overviews:

Occasionally lead criticism overviews to accumulate experiences from your local area. Inquire about the preferences, experiences, and suggestions of users. Utilize the input to direct future updates and upgrades.

12.10 Acknowledgment and Prizes:

Community members who actively contribute, assist others, or produce valuable content should be recognized and rewarded. This could remember highlights for bulletins, hollers via web-based entertainment, or even little awards for extraordinary commitments.

12.11 Customary Updates:

Maintain regular communication with the community regarding game enhancements, new features, and updates. Standard correspondence keeps up with energy and commitment inside the local area.

12.12 Instructive Drives:

Start challenges or educational programs in the community. This could include coding contests, cooperative tasks, or themed learning occasions that line up with the objectives of your coding game.

12.13 Location Concerns Speedily:

Address concerns or issues raised by local area individuals speedily and straightforwardly. Exhibiting responsiveness assembles trust and supports your obligation to the local area's prosperity.

12.14 Work together with Different Drives:

Investigate joint efforts with other instructive drives, coding projects, or associations. Associations can extend your scope and carry assorted points of view to your local area.

Constructing and supporting a lively local area around your coding game requires progressing exertion and commitment. By cultivating a feeling of having a place and shared opportunities for growth, you add to the drawn out progress of your instructive undertaking.

<u>Congrats on making a local area driven space for coding training!</u>

www.ingramcontent.com/pod-product-compliance
Lightning Source LLC
Chambersburg PA
CBHW050047260726

48658CB00005B/1814